Online Dating

CW00765584

Master The Art Of Internet Dating
Create The Best Profile
Choose The Right Pictures
Communication Advice
Finding What You Are Looking For
And Finding Love

By Ace McCloud
Copyright © 2014

Disclaimer

The information provided in this book is designed to provide helpful information on the subjects discussed. The publisher and author are not responsible for anything that may go wrong from the information given in this book. Any references included are provided for informational purposes only. Readers should be aware that any websites or links listed in this book may change.

Table of Contents

DEDICATED TO THOSE WHO ARE PLAYING THE GAME OF LIFE TO

WIN

KEEP ON PUSHING AND NEVER GIVE UP!

Ace McCloud

Be sure to check out my website for all my Books and Audio books.

www.AcesEbooks.com

Introduction

I want to thank you and congratulate you for buying the book, "Ultimate Online and Internet Dating Mastery: Creating The Best Profile, Choosing The Right Pictures, Communication Advice, Finding What You Are Looking For, And Finding Love. "

This book contains proven steps and strategies on how to utilize the internet and dating websites to help you find the perfect partner online. Learn how to effectively take advantage of all the tools at your disposal to give yourself the competitive edge! Learn what works, what to avoid, how to set up a killer profile, what to say in your messages, and much more! There are simple steps and strategies that you can follow that will change online dating from a waste of time to a valuable tool that gives great results!

Chapter 1: The Many Benefits of Online Dating

Before the commercial existence of computers and the World Wide Web, many people had to rely on socializing to find a life partner. Before technology made its mark on the world, many people met their spouses in high school, college, at work, at a bar, or through mutual friends. Today, many people still meet their spouses through these methods. However, as the internet began its incredible rise to fame and more and more people began connecting with each other online, dating websites began to grow in popularity as well. Originally, online dating websites weren't as popular because many people thought they were only for those who couldn't find a date offline. Safety issues also started to become a concern. However, after many people became aware of online safety and after social media websites and mobile apps began to develop, many people now have better attitudes toward online dating—at least 38% of Americans have reported that they have used an online dating website to find a partner.

Although some people may still prefer to meet people offline, there are many benefits to online dating. Online dating is a great option for people who have just moved to a new area or for those who are too shy to go out and meet people. It also benefits people who travel often and those who have busy lives. The ability to select desired qualities in a partner and make specific searches according to personal preferences is highly popular as well.

Online dating also provides people with a sense of security—you don't have to reveal everything about yourself at once to somebody that you meet online—you can reveal things little by little or you can stay completely private until you're ready. Online dating offers you a wide array of choices and you can protect yourself with the help of a "block" function. Best of all, most online dating websites are free. Some of them, like Match.com and eHarmony, charge for their services but offer a wide variety of additional options. You also have a greater chance of finding someone who is seriously looking for a partner from a professional site which costs money. Many mobile developers have also stormed the online dating market, as there are now many dating applications that you can download to your phone or portable devices to stay connected to your dating messages all day long.

Although online dating is an easy and convenient way to meet dates and perhaps your potential spouse, mastering it requires knowledge, effort, practice and technique. It is not as simple as spending five minutes on a dating website and then ending up with your dream date. This book will be your ultimate guide to effectively utilizing online dating websites so that you can get some great results. You will learn how to create the best possible profile, what to include in your first messages, how to make the first couple of dates a success, and how to increase your chances of finding your true love. You will learn the tips and tricks that experts use that will greatly increase your chances of landing that first date and finding your ideal match. All you need to get started is this book, a little patience, and a little determination. Afterward, you will find yourself feeling much more prepared, confident, and ready to begin dating.

Chapter 2: Tips For Building an Excellent Profile

The first step to mastering the art of online dating is to make sure that you know how to build a winning profile. The two best dating websites are eHarmony and Match.com, but there are also many more to explore, such as Plenty Of Fish, OkCupid, Zoosk, Christian Mingle, DateHookup, and more. The purpose of dating websites is to present yourself to other singles so that you can find a potential partner. Your profile is the first thing that your potential dates will see and it's how they will learn more about you. All dating websites have a profile option, where you can add photos of yourself and talk about your personal qualities, values, and interests.

Creating a winning online dating profile is a challenge for both men and women. Many people may think that they can spend five or ten quick minutes making their profile and it will get them lots of attention, but it will not get you the best results. Ideally, you should make your profile a "resume" that brings out your personality, interests, and values. The purpose of an online dating profile is to sell yourself to another person, just as if you were trying to sell yourself to a potential employer. Therefore, it is critical that you make an outstanding profile.

One thing that you need to keep in mind is that there is a huge difference between the amounts of attention you will receive based on whether you are a man or a woman. A woman can put up just an average profile and still get her inbox flooded with messages. For men, it is a whole different story. You will really need to make something special in order to get some attention, and even if you have the greatest profile ever, you are still going to have to put in a good amount of effort contacting women with intelligent messages, otherwise you are unlikely to see any good results. To put this in perspective, a woman can make a nice profile and in one month easily get over two hundred messages from all sorts of men. On the other hand, a guy can make a nice profile, and over a month it is not uncommon for him to not get a single message from a woman.

I used to be extremely frustrated by this. I couldn't understand why women wouldn't contact me. I had a nice profile, college degree, fit, healthy, good family and friends, etc. But over several years, I think I had one, maybe two women go out of their way to message me. Now I did get plenty of messages from scam artists, women with beautiful pictures and saying all the right things that a guy wants to hear. You will have to watch out for this. While internet dating has cleaned up in the last several years, beware of anyone who sends you messages with a hidden profile or an incomplete profile. Especially if they want to contact you outside of the dating site. These are scam artists, so be wary.

So after a lot of frustration, I decided to do some research. One critical piece of information that I found out was that if you live near a large city, it makes it much more difficult to date online. The amount of messages women will receive from all sorts of men goes up tremendously near cities. I personally live right between Baltimore and Washington, so if I search for women within thirty miles it covers both of those massive cities and everything in between. So the competition is just incredible. I talked to several women and asked them how many messages they were getting, and the result just blew my mind. They were getting at least ten messages a day, and some were getting over fifty messages per day, to the point where they would just build up in their inbox! So to be successful in high competition areas like this you will need to put in the work to be successful. With this in mind, below are some great tips for building an attention grabbing and intriguing profile.

Tip #1: Don't Start Off Alone

Get a close friend to help you fill your profile out. This is especially a good tip for those who are shy. A good friend will help you figure out what your best qualities are, as many times he or she knows you better than yourself. Having a friend help you out will also prevent you from coming off as narcissistic or conceited. A friend can help you point out your strengths, good qualities, the funny things about you, and the wonderful things about you. When picking a friend to help you fill out your profile, try to choose someone who you have known for a very long time. This way, they can differentiate between your short-term qualities and long-term qualities. You can say something like this: My friends say that my best qualities are...

Tip #2: Highlight Your Personality

Be descriptive about yourself. Research has found that both men and women think the most important quality about a potential partner is personality, followed by looks, sense of humor, and education. Avoid describing yourself with generic terms such as "funny," "nice," or "caring." Your personality will naturally emulate those qualities. In addition, think about all the other men and women who use those terms as well. The trick is to really stand out and make yourself unique (because you are!).

Using unique adjectives will make you come off as exciting and interesting instead of redundant and boring. For example, instead of describing yourself as "caring," you could say that you love helping others or volunteering at a local animal shelter. This way, if there is another person who likes to volunteer helping out others, your profile will catch his or her attention. Also avoid using generic descriptions for your hobbies, such as "watching movies" or "traveling." There are many people all over the world who like to do those things. Think of ways to make your hobbies specific and descriptive so that you can find somebody who likes the same things as you.

Tip #3: Your Profile Headline

This is one of the most important parts of your profile. Be sure to spend some time on this so that you come up with something really great. Since the headline is one of the first things people will see when viewing your profile, it needs to be good. One great strategy is to make your headline playful and humorous. Playful and humorous headlines have a much higher click through rate. You can also pose your headline as a question, with the only way to see the answer is by clicking through to see your profile. Keep the headline positive, try and avoid any negative words, and try to be as intriguing as possible so that people will want to click and read your profile. If you are having trouble coming up with a headline on your own, simply put "dating headlines" into your local internet browser to reveal hundreds of possibilities. Be sure to stay away from overly sexual or ridiculous headlines. You want to come up with three or four good headlines, and switch them up every 2 to 3 weeks to keep your profile looking fresh.

Tip #4: Avoid Negative Phrases

Do not try to separate likely candidates from unlikely candidates. For example, do not write phrases such as "do not contact me if you still live at home." Phrases like that will make you come off as negative or high maintenance and will turn many people away. They will focus more on wondering what you're going to hate about them than what you are going to like about them. After a quick glance of picky and negative profiles like this, the first thing most people will do is delete it and move onto the next. Resist the urge to write about what you don't want in your profile and dedicate a little more patience to evaluating every candidate individually as they come along. You can always hit the "delete" or "block" button, or simply ignore the message if you don't like the profile. For every 10 duds that you may find, you may end up finding someone really great by simply giving them a chance.

Tip #5: Don't Lie

Be honest, but not too honest. For example, you do not have to tell your life story on your profile. Try not to include details that may sound "off," such as having to take depression medications or having to overcome image issues. You should save those details for when you really meet the right person, and even then not until after the third date. You should be honest about topics like your values, your short-term and long-term goals, and your interests. On the same token, do not lie about anything, either. Studies show that the top three things that men lie about are their age, height, and income while women tend to lie about their weight, build, and age. Stand out from the crowd and be honest in your profile. This will work out better for you in the long run.

Tip #6: Stay Positive

Be positive about yourself. If you cannot love yourself, it will be very hard for another person to love you. If you talk about yourself in a negative tone, it is more likely to turn off people than attract them. Again, think of it as if you were applying for a job—don't write anything about yourself that a potential employer wouldn't approve of. Most people are only going to spend a short amount of time evaluating your profile, so don't give them any reason to delete it after a quick browse.

Tip #7: Create a Winning User Name

Some dating websites allow you to create a user name to go with your profile. Make sure that you create an excellent, catchy user name that will attract people to your profile. For example, do not use anything boring like "singleperson111" or anything desperate like "givinguphope34343." Instead, have some fun with it and make it reflect your personality. Many people like to include their nicknames or interests in their user name. Also, do not make it too vulgar, otherwise some people may be turned off and under the impression that you're just interested in hooking up. Try and find a username that describes your personality in a positive light. For example: Love_Nature, Ballroom_Dancer, Playful_Musician, Fitness_Lover, etc. Your username is critically important, so take your time and find something you really like. If you can naturally tie your username into your profile headline, that will help increase the strength of your profile.

Tip #8: Keep It Simple For Women, Longer For Men

If you are a woman, when writing out your dating profile do not make it too long. While many women enjoy reading long things, most men don't. Limit yourself to 3-4 short paragraphs. Most of the time, men will not bother to read anything that is too long. Think of it as writing an elevator pitch for yourself—if you only had enough time to ride an elevator from the bottom of a building to the top, what would you say? On the other hand, men will need to put a lot more effort into their profile. With the incredible competition out there to be noticed by women, your profile should be at least 6-8 paragraphs long.

Tip #9: Check Your Spelling/Grammar

Although it may not seem important, bad spelling and grammar is a huge turnoff for many people. Always proofread your content, even if you're the greatest speller in the world. Even the best writers make mistakes. You can simply write out a rough draft in a word processor and use the spell-check option to check it. Read it over several times to make sure that it is clear and coherent. You can even ask a friend to read it over to make sure that it's well written and even get some good advice. It is estimated that 30% of men who use the word "whom" are more likely to get more attention from women than those who don't.

Tips Especially For Men

Tip #10: Avoid Selfies

Studies have found that most men found "selfies" or pictures you take of yourself, attractive for women, but most women did not approve of male selfies. There are more tips and tricks for selecting pictures, which will be covered in Chapter 3.

Tip #11: Use the Word "Women" Instead of "Girls"

Men who refer to women as "women" and not "girls" or a similar synonym had a 28% higher chance of getting more messages from women. Keep this in mind when filling out your profile or messaging other women. It may help you stand out from the crowd.

Tip #12: Mention Your Interest In Sports

Men who mention the sports surfing, yoga, skiing, golf, biking, running, and hiking got more attention than those who listed basketball, baseball, or kickball as their sports of interest. Surfing ranked the highest and running ranked last on the highest list. If you're not good at one of those sports, it is a good opportunity to mention that you might like to learn one. It can serve as a great conversation starter and if you find a woman who is interested in learning the same sport, you already have a potential date night. For women, yoga ranked the highest and biking ranked the lowest on the list. Women also listed dancing and tennis as their favorite sports interests.

Tip #13: Disengage Yourself From Gender Roles

Men who used keywords about children for their interests in their profile got more responses than those who listed their interests with keywords such as "electronics," or "cars." Interestingly, women who mentioned their interest in "electronics," or a male-oriented activity got more responses than if they listed their interests as children.

Tip #14: Career and Retirement

Men who use the keyword "retirement" concerning their career and work in their profile are more likely to get responses than those who don't use that word. Interestingly, it is the second most unattractive keyword in a woman's profile. Also, men and women who portray their career in a positive light in their profile had higher response rates.

Tips Especially For Women

Tip #15: Switch Your Default Profile Picture Often

Women who tend to change their default profile picture often can increase their chances of getting responses. By changing your default profile picture, men who passed you over the first time are more likely to give you a second look when they do not see the same picture continuously.

Tip #16: Make Yourself Open to New Experiences

Having higher levels of openness has a direct correlation with getting more responses. For example, if you are open to learning how to ski and you come across a man who is an avid skier, you not only have a conversation starter and a common interest but you also have a potential date.

Tip #17: Know Which Body Parts Men Are Attracted Too

Studies show that men are most interested in a woman's stomach, arms, legs, butts, and feet. The most popular hair colors that men like to see on women are blonde, brown, and black, although a good number of men don't mind what your hair color is. Knowing this can be helpful in selecting pictures to post.

Tip #18: Know How to Present Yourself

Although it may seem like men are only attracted to your looks, almost half of men prefer a woman who is on the modern career path. 34% of men prefer the "girl next door" look and 24% prefer the "hottie" look. On the other side, most women prefer the "nice guy" type while the second most popular preference is a mixture of "nice guy and bad guy."

Tip #19: Prove that You Will Fit in With His Friends

One of the things that men find most attractive is the ability to fit in with his friends. That's not to say that you have to act like a man, but if you can get along with his guy friends and know how to have fun with them, a man will be more likely to want to date you. Fitting in with a man and his friends also means that you will likely form a solid friendship, which is the foundation for any successful relationship.

Tip #20: Don't Sweat Little Details

It's pretty obvious that men dislike nagging and complaining, so if you can present yourself in a way that shows you don't sweat little details, you're most likely to get more hits and find somebody who is right for you.

Tip #21: Send Out A Few Messages

As mentioned earlier, it is extremely rare for a man can be contacted by a woman on a dating website. Just like women like to feel important, men do as well. Women can greatly increase their chances of finding someone special by doing some profile searches on their own and contacting the men they like. The majority of men will be extremely flattered by this and you will immediately put yourself to the top of the list.

Tip #22: Don't Appear To Be High Maintenance or Money Hungry

One of the most unattractive qualities a woman can have is to appear to be high maintenance or money hungry. If your profile is filled with all the fabulous destinations you want to travel to, all the fine dining areas you want to go to, or all the fashionable clothes you want to wear, that is a quick way to turn off most men. Instead of thinking about what a great woman you are, the first thing a man is going to think is: "My goodness this woman's going to cost me a fortune!" and move onto the next profile.

More Tips For Men And Women

Tip #22: Using Popular Keywords In Your Profile

There are certain words that generate a lot of attention and will increase your chances of being matched up. Some of the more popular words you may want to consider sprinkling throughout your profile are: Family, Friends, Cooking, Dancing, Helping other people, The Beach, Traveling, Animal lover, Music, Laughter and Humor, Art, Fitness, The Park, Health, and Being Social.

Tip #23: Don't Come Across As Needy

Being seen as needy can be unattractive to both men and women, try and keep your profile as upbeat and strong as possible.

Tip #24: Be Mysterious

Don't tell everything about yourself in the profile. Just say enough to get the other person interested and wanting to know more.

Tip #25: Check Out The Competition

It is a good idea to search other men's or other women's profiles to see what they are doing and what you may like. This should give you several good ideas that you can easily add to your own profile.

Tip #26: Call To Action

Be sure to end your profile by asking to hear from the reader. For example, the last sentences of your profile should be something like: "Congratulations on making it to the end. Enough reading, I would love to hear from you! Simply click the button to contact me now!" The goal is to encourage as many people as possible to reach out and send you a message after reading your profile.

Chapter 3: Attract More Dates By Choosing the Best Profile Pictures

Making sure that you choose the best pictures of yourself for your online dating portfolio is another key step in mastering online dating. The photos you select for your profile will play a big difference in whether you receive many messages or not, so you want to make sure you select the best ones. It may be tempting to not post any pictures of yourself at all, but research shows that online dating profiles with pictures are nine times more likely to receive attention. They serve as a great visual aid to highlighting your hobbies, interests, and personality.

There are some more statistics that will convince you to upload your best shots. One study found that those who uploaded four or more pictures of themselves in 2013 got the most hits from other users. 67% of the time, men reached out to and started a conversation with women who uploaded at least four pictures of themselves. Another study found that the best kinds of shots were those that showed at least half of your body, as opposed to extreme close ups. The same study showed that pictures that obviously showed another person cut-out were most likely to get less hits, with the assumption that the cut-out person is your ex. Finally, pictures that are blurry, small, or hard to see will also not get you much attention.

So what kind of pictures should you upload to make the most out of your online dating experience? Although everybody will have different preferences and opinions, the following are some general tips that you should follow to get the best results.

Be sure to include pictures of yourself smiling. Studies show that a person's smile and appearance is the second most important factor on first dates, right behind personality. Men find happy, smiling women more attractive because it shows receptiveness and femininity. Women find men who look prideful of their appearance attractive because it gives off the sense of masculinity and the ability to take care of a family. Interestingly, you should try to include pictures of yourself that show the left side of your face. We tend to display our emotions with the left side of our face. Here's a quick-fix tip: if you have a really great, high-quality picture of yourself smiling but it focuses on the right side of your face, simply flip it around in a picture editor. Check out this YouTube video Pleated-Jeans Youtube Channel by to learn how to take natural smiling pictures: How to Smile Naturally for Photos.

Try to include pictures of yourself that were taken outside. Pictures with excellent lighting tend to attract more people and the best kind of light is natural light. Include any great pictures of yourself that were taken at a park, beach, lake, or any other nature spot. Be aware, however, that bright sunlight will cause too many shadows and can make you appear older. The best kind of natural light for taking pictures is during the evening, when the sun is not directly above you.

Check out this YouTube video on How to use natural light and fill flash with digital photography by Tony Northrup to learn how to take the best pictures outside.

Make sure that your pictures show that you're dressed to impress. Avoid using photos of yourself when you're wearing lavish patterns or lots of accessories because they take away from the true subject—you. The best kinds of clothes to wear are one-toned, bright colors. They will make you stand out against your background. For men, try and have one picture where you are wearing red, studies have shown that women like this.

Taking flirty profile pictures may seem provocative but research suggests that they can attract just as much attention as a regular head-shot picture. For men and women, it is best to flirt directly into your camera for the best results. Try to avoid making a flirty face while looking away from the camera. Furthermore, the same research suggested that the "Myspace angle" shot (where you hold the camera above your face and take the picture yourself) also got women the most attention, even without showing any skin. For men specifically, most women find it attractive when they pose with their friends. If possible, choose a picture where you are in the center, this will increase the power of the image. Also, for men and women, be sure to include one photo when you're dressed up in a nice suit or dress.

For men, avoid topless photos and posing with babies or children. Although instinctively we think that this would be attractive to women, oddly enough it is not. So try and avoid shirtless photos and no photos with children or babies. If you have a really great body, try to show it off while wearing a nice tight t-shirt.

You should also post pictures of yourself doing something interesting—it can be anything from playing a guitar, to skiing, to shooting a cross-bow. These types of pictures are more likely to engage people and encourage them to strike up a conversation with you. Finally, make sure your face is showing. This tip may seem obvious but often times, people post pictures of inanimate objects, animals, their children, or of something that that is not them.

Although many dating websites, such as Match.com, allow you to upload many pictures, try to keep it simple and only upload four to six. By uploading too many pictures of yourself, you can possibly come off as conceited or arrogant. Show off your best pictures, and you can always show some more pictures later on in messages.

Take the best pictures of yourself using a digital camera. Cell phone cameras and built-in computer webcams take okay pictures, but by using a digital camera with a high megapixel rating, you can really bring out your best features. You can easily download pictures taken on a digital camera to your computer. You might also consider investing in a webcam if you plan on doing any video chatting.

Many computers and laptops come with a bulit-in webcam, but some do not. Also, some of the built-in webcams do not have a good picture quality.

Chapter 4: The First Messages

Once you have created a great profile, it's time for some action. After searching through some profiles and finding one that you like and would like to contact, it comes time for the first message. This is a critical area that many people do not put enough effort into. Your first message is extremely important, so you need to do it right. First messages that are extremely short, have misspelled words, are too forward, sound creepy, are hard to understand, etc. are very likely to be quickly ignored. Timing is important as well. Studies have shown that the best times to contact someone is between 6:30pm and 8:30pm in the evening, and that anytime during the day on Sunday is the best time to send a message.

You want the first message to be pleasant. Starting off by giving a nice compliment about the other persons profile is a good way to start. It lets the other person know that you took the time to actually read their profile, and it also shows that you are considerate. Try and make a unique message to each person you are writing to. If you are simply sending the same message to a bunch of different people, it usually does not work that well. Try and stand out from the crowd by putting in the time to analyze the other persons profile and talk about a few interests that you both have in common, or something interesting in their profile that you liked. After giving a nice compliment, take a few sentences or a paragraph and tell the other person a little bit about yourself.

Make the first message about 2-4 paragraphs. Your goal is to get the conversation going rather than having your message ignored. The nice thing about internet dating is that you have lots of search parameters that you can use to find who you are looking for. So instead of relying on your daily matches alone, put the effort into searching for someone that you really like. This way you are not wasting all your time contacting someone who really isn't your ideal match.

In the first message it is ok to tease a little bit, but always appear to be non-threatening. Do not mention anything sexually explicit on the first message, or brag about things in your life. It is also a good idea to avoid CAPS, try and avoid abbreviations that the other person may not understand, and use LOL's and smiley faces sparingly. Another great idea is to ask a question on your first message. Your main goal of the first message is to get a response. So an intelligent question about something they are interested in usually works quite well.

When ending your first message, be sure to let them know that you would like to hear back from them.

If the first message is successful and you get the conversation started, you are half way there! So put in the extra effort that 95% of the other people won't put in to send a great first message and really start seeing some great results!

The Conversation Has Started

Once you have started a dialogue, you are in a great position. Usually one or both people are very excited about their new potential match. So it is critical not to do anything stupid to mess things up at this point. If you think that you really like this person, your goal is to have a nice, easy going conversation that will lead to a first date. Don't make the other person wait a long time to hear back from you. Waiting a long time can cause the excitement to die down. You want to get the conversation going being as intelligent and thoughtful as possible.

After a nice exchange of messages it is usually a good time for the guy to ask the woman if she would like to chat on the phone, on live chat, on Skype, etc. This is my favorite part of the dating process. This is where you'll really be able to get a good idea of the other person. I am always wary of someone who will refuse to talk on the phone or live chat. If they refuse to do this, it is hard to take that person seriously as a potential match. Talking on the phone or voice chat is a great tool for women as well, as you will generally be able to tell what type of guy you are dealing with just after a short chat.

The goal of the conversation should be to simply get to know each other better. If the connection is just like crazy good, you can chat for quite a long time. But generally, it is best to just keep the chat going for about 15 to 30 minutes and then end the conversation on a positive note, hopefully with an agreement to meet up for a date in the next week or so. Once again, it is not a good idea to play games or make the other person wait a long time. With love, it is generally best to strike when the iron is hot and see where fate will lead you. Given too much time, the brain can come up with all sorts of negative things that are not conducive with finding love.

Chapter 5: Making The First 3 Dates Count

Once you have made a connection and scored that first date, it is time to hopefully have a great time. Tip: research shows that women prefer men to ask them out and many men do not prefer women to ask them out first. By knowing how to effectively communicate with your date on the first couple of dates, you will stand a better chance of getting to know him or her. When it comes to online dating and looking for a long-term relationship, the second date is almost always harder to get than the first.

Note For Women Concerned With Safety: Before you arrange any in-person meetings with a person you met online, it is important to review the rules of online dating safety. You should always get to know the person online before you agree to meet them offline. One way to check a person out is to type their name into a search engine or invest in a background check. A background check often costs money but it could end up saving your life. Always meet a person in a busy, public place and always tell a friend where you are going. Do not drink or do drugs or otherwise let yourself become impaired. Also, you should provide your own transportation to and from the first date. If you are traveling a long distance to meet someone, stay in your own hotel room and utilize public transportation. As always, you should always trust your instincts.

The First Date

The first date is always a challenge, especially if you are meeting somebody in person for the first time. However, there are easy ways to get around the anxiety of meeting somebody new. Whether you are meeting for dinner or just getting together for coffee, there are plenty of tips you can follow to increase your chances of getting a second date, granted that you both get along well. When you first meet the person, be sure to look them directly in the eye and smile. Studies have shown that if you look away even for a split second, it immediately lowers the attraction level.

The things that happen on a first date are usually pretty basic. You should always be honest about yourself, just as you are on your online profile. You can ask good conversation-starting questions such as, "what do you enjoy doing on your days off," or "what are your values?" These questions aren't too personal but they will give you a good idea of what kind of person you are on a date with. Be careful to make sure that you are actually listening to your date's answers and not busy trying to think of your next question while he or she is answering. If you need to brush up on your listening skills, check out Fig ESSA's YouTube video, Effective Listening Skills, for a refresher. After a while, you should become engaged in a deep conversation. Most importantly, remember to show good body language. Make eye contact with your date, smile, and lean towards him or her. If you have a really good connection with your date, chances are your body language will naturally occur—a good sign.

However, there are some things that you should avoid on the first date. Avoid serious questions that concern religion, money, children, or politics. Do not try to be funny or anything else besides yourself. For women, allow men to pay for your meal if you go out to dinner. If you're truly insistent about paying for your own meal, work it out beforehand, otherwise it may place you in an awkward position. When I was in High School, I had a first date go poorly because my mom told me I had to pay for the first date, and when the girl insisted on paying for her movie ticket three times in a row I felt insulted and it basically messed up the date from that point forward. To this day I don't like movies as a first date. A good strategy is to offer to let the woman pay the tip if she really wants to contribute on a dining date, or letting her know that she can contribute on the next date id she would like. Once you know each other better, then splitting the bill is totally fine, but on a first date this is a good rule to follow.

For men, don't let yourself become distracted by the waitress. Your date will notice and it won't look good for you. **Don't drink much or at all on your first date and don't talk about your exes in the past—those two things can wait until you really get to know the other person.** Even if the other person brings up the topic or wants to drink heavily, find some way to change the subject and stay sober yourself. I've fallen into the trap of talking about exes on a first date a few times myself and it has never worked out well. Keep the conversation light, focusing on intelligent questions about the other person and their interests.

Finally, don't give up too soon. Love is not always at first sight and it often takes time to get to know someone. If you believe that your first date went well and you'd like to pursue a relationship, do not be afraid to ask for a second date. Check out this YouTube video Yikes! Avoid Making These First Date Faux Pas At All Costs by YourTango for some reinforcing tips on the do's and don'ts of your first date.

Remember that it is best to meet somebody sooner rather than later, otherwise your potential date may begin to think that you are not interested. Talking online and on the phone are good ways to keep the conversation going after the first date.

Another good strategy is to just meet for a coffee instead of going out for a meal. Beverage dates are typically shorter than lunch/dinner dates and it will give you enough time to decide if you think the two of you will be a good match. Finally, avoid taking your date out to your favorite coffee house or restaurant. If it just so happens that your first date doesn't lead to a second, you stand a higher chance of running into that same person on another date in the same spot—an awkward situation.

Here are some other great first dates ideas to help you get started:

- Take a nice walk

- Take a class that you would both enjoy
- Check out an aquarium, zoo, or national park
- Help each other shop for something you need
- Meet for coffee
- Have a great lunch or dinner
- Hike, rock climb, or engage in another physical activity
- Play a card or board game
- Check out any local historic sites

The Second Date

When it comes to the second date, you will still need to do some preparing to make it successful. First and foremost, you should communicate to each other to make sure that you both want to pursue a second date. Sometimes, you might have a horrible time but your date will think otherwise and ask you out again. If you don't think there's a connection, just say so. Don't lead your date on. However, if you both had an equal amount of fun on the first date, then by all means, accept the second date. For an added touch, send your date a message thanking them for a good time.

Remember, it's still the second date, so continue to keep personal matters private. It is also a good idea not to have sexual relations yet. For men, continue to be yourself to make your date feel comfortable. On the second date, you want to get to know the other person a little better. Some great second date ideas are lunch or dinner dates, a movie date, an arcade date, or do something outdoors, such as taking a walk in the park. The key is to remember to keep the activity fun and light.

The second date is a key time for men to make an impression on their dates. Women love it when men can memorize something that they said, so if your date mentioned that she loved to read, bring it up and you'll make a lasting impression. You can begin to compliment her, as long as you don't overdo it. Try to limit yourself to giving her three compliments to start. Also, many girls actually don't like it when men bring gifts on the second date. It often makes them feel uncomfortable, so instead, give her a compliment or just show her that you're enjoying your time with her.

For women, it is much safer to travel to your second date with your date. Now that you've seen that they are a real, normal person, you will most likely feel much safer traveling with them. You can begin to take small steps to developing chemistry by lightly touching your date at times, just enough to make them want to be with you. Also take the opportunity to talk about your first date on your second date. You can talk about the things that went well, which will strengthen your connection. Finally, don't have any expectations. Remind yourself that it is only the second date and you are still getting time to know each other.

Here is a list of some great second date ideas:

- Attend a social function together (church, community party, etc)
- Go to a comedy or jazz club
- Hit a retro arcade or go to the boardwalk
- Attend a concert
- Go on another nature walk
- Watch a sporting event
- Go Bowling
- Check out a museum

If all goes well on both ends for the second date, then talk to each other about setting up a third date. Again, make sure that the decision to meet for a third date is mutual. Check out this YouTube video on How to Get a Second Date by TrippAdvice.com for some extra tips on how to make your second date successful.

The Third Date

Once you have made it to your third date, it is safe to say that you and your date may have the potential for an exclusive relationship. Often times, the third date is the one where you will know if you really want to pursue your date. As always, be yourself on this date, more than ever.

Your first and second dates may have only lasted for a few hours, but you should try spending a bit more time with each other on this one. You can take a drive to the country and have a picnic lunch or take a day trip to the city—whatever you choose to do, try to spend most of the day together. Another really good idea is to go to a theme park together for the day. Most theme parks have scary roller coasters, romantic rides, and fun things to do, like game booths. For men, the third date is a good time to kiss your date when she first arrives. It is also acceptable to hold hands or cuddle on the third date. The third date is a good time to come clean on some things that you may have been holding back on, but nothing too deep. If you really like your date, now is the time to let them now. Either by subtle touching and caressing, nice words, positive body language, or a passionate end of date kiss.

Here are some excellent third date ideas that you can use:

- Take a road trip to a nearby state or city
- Go to an amusement park
- Have a movie night together
- Go out to dinner
- Browse a flea market
- Have a picnic
- Go dancing

Even though it's already your third date, still try to focus on having fun rather than trying to have sex. If you're going to be together in the long-run, sex can wait until you've both established a solid friendship. However, if it feels right, then definitely go for it. You may never get another chance. Like mentioned several times earlier, with love, it is best not to wait. If you know... you know. I would say that with the majority of the true love girlfriends I have had, the connection was pretty quick and powerful. So don't be afraid to try and turn that spark into a roaring fire!

If you are still having doubts by your third date, then your date probably isn't the right match for you. Check out this YouTube video by Ask Doctor Paul for some more tips on how to make your third date a success: What Can I Expect On A Third Date.

So, when is it appropriate to talk about your past? Talking about issues such as your relationship history or major life challenges is a fragile activity but it's not always a bad thing—talking about your feelings on these issues with your new partner can help you determine what you want to get out of your *new* relationship. The key is to know the right time to do it.

When you're preparing to have sexual intercourse with your new partner, you might want to consider giving him or her a basic history of your sexual relations. If you have had sexual intercourse with many other people, without protection, or have contracted an STD, your partner has a right to know. While it is sometimes important to reveal your past sexual relations, you don't necessarily have to go into details. This YouTube video, How To Talk About Past Relationships by HowToWebVidz, is helpful for figuring out when it's safe to talk about your detailed relationship history.

When it comes to past personal issues, the timing to talk about them is up to you. For example, if you once struggled with depression or had a serious illness, wait until you know and trust your partner before telling him or her about the details. Only disclose details to somebody that you know and trust. Trust is key, because if you don't want your partner to spread information about a sensitive subject, you will have to know that they will keep it private before you share it with them. The best time to reveal things like these is to wait until you're truly comfortable with each other.

When it comes to talking about sensitive or past topics, you can set some ground rules with each other. You can both agree on how much or how little you want to share with each other. Try not to talk too much about your ex-partners to avoid making your current partners feel insecure. Also, try not to be too secretive when your partner asks about your past—it may cause you to come off as sketchy and not trustworthy. Answer each other's questions while reminding each other that the past is in the past.

Chapter 6: How To Develop a Long-Term Relationship Via Online Dating

While many people use online dating sites to find hook-ups and short-term relationships, many people use online dating sites to ultimately find somebody to spend the rest of their lives with. When it comes to looking for a long-term relationship through online dating sites, it will likely take some time and effort before you find somebody who you connect with. However, there are some ways that you can make this process easier.

Be sure to check into what kind of relationship your date is looking for. Luckily, most online dating sites have sections in each profile that allows you to state what kind of relationship you want. If your potential date has "looking to meet new friends" or "short-term" or something similar in that section of their profile, the odds of developing a long-term relationship with him or her is slim. However, if they list that they are looking for a long-term relationship or just a relationship, you have a much better chance.

Some online dating websites also have an option where users can list the length of their last or longest relationship. This is another good way to figure out if someone may be interested in a long-term relationship or not. For example, if somebody lists their last relationship as lasting for five years, he or she may still need time to heal from that relationship before even thinking about jumping into another long-term relationship.

Finally, look for signs in their pictures and their interests. Although you cannot always tell what a person is like based off the reputation they make for themselves, if you see keywords like "love to party" or "always looking for a good time," and many pictures in bars, clubs, or other party settings, there is a good chance that a long-term relationship is not in that person's near future.

Some people may be under the impression that online dating is only for those who are looking for casual relationships. However, 29% of people in the United States have reported to knowing somebody who met their partner online and got married. The trick to finding a long-term relationship online has many steps. First and foremost, you should use some of the strategies mentioned above to figure out who is worth talking too and who isn't. Then, you should try to find people who share common interests, hobbies, and values with you. As long as you follow the steps from Chapters 2 and 3 in creating the best profile, this should be a bit easier. Then, you should follow the steps in Chapter 5 to make the most out of your first three dates.

Once you have gotten this far, you likely have the potential to form a long-term relationship with your partner. There are several strategies that you can implement to develop a healthy, long-term relationship with the possibility of marriage.

Communication in any relationship is key. If you cannot communicate clearly with your partner, you will not be on the same page and it will be much harder to make the relationship work. Use some of the upcoming tips to strengthen your communication with your partner for a healthy, long-lasting relationship.

While it may be tempting to start talking dirty to each other or having sex early on, you should really try to save it until you both know each other well. If you jump into foreplay and sex too early, it can be distracting from the other important parts of your relationship that you have to work on, such as developing friendship, trust, and communication. If you're really committed to developing a long-term, permanent relationship, you might even talk to your partner about saving yourselves for a longer-than-usual time. Check out themaleroomtv's YouTube video How Long Should I Wait to have sex for some great tips on this.

Instead of focusing on the bedroom, focus on your life goals and values. Ask yourselves if you both want the same kind of life. If you want to settle down and live in a big house one day and your partner wants to travel the world, it is better to figure that out sooner rather than later. The point of marriage is to grow old together, not grow apart from each other, so it is best to establish your goals with each other early on.

Try not to spend *too* much time together at first. Although it may be tempting, you should take small steps and work on developing your relationship. Spending too much time together in the beginning or even moving in with each other right away is a recipe for disaster. Remind yourself that by only seeing each other a few times a week instead of every night, you can appreciate the company of each other more. Best of all, if you take small steps in the beginning, you can eventually move in with each other and then you will get to spend every day together then. Try to think of it as a long-term goal with the ultimate reward.

On that note, when you *do* spend time with each other, make sure it is in person and as personal as possible. For example, instead of talking to each other on a social media website, you could call or get together. Instead of leaving each other messages on Facebook, you could text each other. Keeping your relationship as personal as possible increases the chances that the two of you will become close, and it saves yourselves from any social media drama, especially if your messages are public. This will help you practice great communication.

Set ground rules, boundaries, and standards at the very beginning. If you do not make what you want known and how you want to be treated clear, you may feel trapped or vulnerable down the road and it will be harder to fix your relationship in the future. Establishing communication is one of the top strategies in forming a successful relationship. This is also a good way to see what kind of person your partner really is.

After you have spent some time together, ask yourself if you trust your partner and feel safe with him or her. If you are afraid to communicate your feelings to him or her, then you should probably rethink your relationship. However, if your partner is the type of person whom you can tell anything to, then you likely have a better chance at being together in the long-term. You can try to determine this early-on by becoming aware of how your partner treats other people.

Remember that no relationship is 100% perfect. We all have our flaws and our strong points. Ask yourself if you are willing to see past any flaws in your partner and figure out if your partner is willing to do the same for you. Weigh out the pros and the cons of your relationship. If the pros outweigh the cons, then you are on the path to having a strong and healthy relationship. Never develop a long-term relationship with somebody with the mindset that you are going to help them change.

Finally, the most important strategy for forming a long-term relationship is to be yourself and have some fun. It may seem obvious, but by being yourself, you have a better chance at feeling more secure and comfortable in your relationship. If you have to act differently around your partner, you will soon get tired of having to pretend and your relationship will suffer. Do not get discouraged by any letdowns or mistakes. We all learn from mistakes and you often have to make some before you get on the right track.

Chapter 7: How To Find Your True Love

What could be a better dream come true than finding your true love? It happens in the movies and on the TV all the time and it can happen in real life too. Many people make the mistake of thinking that true love can happen overnight, but it actually takes plenty of skills, practice, and preparation. This chapter provides some useful tips to help you ready yourself for finding your true love when it comes into your life.

Overcome Insecurity

One mistake that many people make in their relationships is that they become dependent on their partner. In other words, instead of focusing on how to appreciate their partner's love and company, they tend to focus more on trying *not* to lose them, which often backfires. One way to find your true love is to understand the importance of independence and self-identification. Before you can even think about finding your true love, make yourself your true love first. Learn how to live independently and learn how to love yourself, regardless of your flaws. By doing this, you will become much more secure and confident in a relationship, instead of always trying to rely on someone else to fulfill your needs. If you can find somebody who has the same self-loving attitude, then you are really in business for a successful relationship.

Don't Settle

Settling in a relationship too early or too fast is probably one of the top mistakes that many people make in trying to find their true love. If you have been with somebody for a long time but you cannot be yourself, you don't have common interests and values, or if you just don't get along, it can be hard to admit that you're not right for each other. Don't settle with somebody just because you've been with them for a long time or because it's convenient. This can hold you back from finding the person that you're supposed to be with. If you make sure that you are an independent person before you get involved in any relationship, it is often easier to realize this and get out.

Don't Be Too Picky

We all have our ideal idea of our soul mate: maybe they are smart and rich or maybe they are good looking and funny. However, we must remind ourselves that nobody and no relationship is 100% perfect. Instead of waiting to find the perfect partner, ask yourself what factors are the most important for you in a partner. Then ask yourself what things you would be willing to look past in a person if you want to be in a long-term relationship with him or her. Be logical and realistic when it comes to this—for example, if you've found somebody who enjoys the same things that you do but they snore too much, you might consider looking past their snoring problem. A bad example would be dumping someone because they are not taller than you, even though you have the same values. It can be very easy to spend years and decades trying to find that fairy tale perfect person, only to realize that you have been too picky and that you let an ideal match get away.

Forgive Your Past Partners

Another crucial step that is essential in finding your true love is to forgive your past partners. Let go of any grudges that you've been holding against them and even apologize if you've truly wronged them. It will eliminate any emotional baggage that you are carrying around and you will feel relieved, better, and able to move on.

Don't Look For Love

Although this entire book has been about looking for love on the internet, there are two ways of "looking" for love. Looking for love online by creating a profile and making yourself available is the right way to look for love. The wrong way to look for love is to talk to somebody for a few days and then automatically jump into a relationship or expect a relationship. I like to believe that you will find your true love without even realizing it at first, or expecting it to happen. When you "catch" yourself falling for somebody that you've talked too for a while, chances are that they can be your true love.

Don't Be Shy

Shyness is a big reason people lose out on finding their true love. Shyness makes us nervous around new people, when we are in new situations, and it also causes us to stay quiet. To find your true love, you will have to talk to new people and be open to new opportunities. If you consider yourself a shy person, you should try to overcome your shyness. The first step to overcoming shyness is to think positively about yourself, a tip that I mentioned earlier. You can also have a positive attitude toward your shyness. For example, tell yourself that you *can* overcome your shyness. You can also practice deep breathing exercises to help yourself feel more relaxed in unfamiliar situations. If you truly have trouble overcoming your shyness, you can look into Hypnosis Therapy.

Have Faith

Some people believe that there is a right match for everyone. Other people do not believe that a true love actually exists. Again, keeping in mind that no relationship is 100% perfect, sometimes having faith and beliefs can keep you motivated. If you keep a positive attitude and firmly believe that there is somebody out there for you, you will be less likely to give up searching for your match and less likely to settle with somebody who isn't right.

Ask Yourself the Ultimate Question: Does My Partner Make Me Want to be a Better Person?

If your partner makes you want to improve your life and become a better person than you already are, then you probably have found someone who is your true love. Note that if your partner constantly makes demands of you to change yourself, that is not a good sign. Your partner should inspire you to make positive aspects of yourself even more positive. For example, if your partner is concerned about your lung health, he or she may inspire you to quit smoking. You should also try to encourage your partner to become a better person as well. A relationship in which you want to bring out the best in each other, not the worst, is a great sign that you are meant for each other.

When talking to people online and meeting them in real life, keep these tips in mind, especially if you've made it past the third date. It takes work from each person in the relationship to make true love happen. If your partner is willing to work with you, then you've got yourself an excellent relationship. Overall, stay positive, confident, and knowledgeable, and you can have your very own happy ending.

Conclusion

I hope this book was able to help you to help you get a head start with online dating so that you can have some fun dating and eventually find the love of your life.

The next step is to put what you've learned into practice. Take a look at some of the best dating websites mentioned in this book and create a profile. Take some new pictures of yourself and put in the effort to making an incredible profile using the advice given in this book. Make sure you have a good user name and headline, and that you are sending quality messages to people you would actually like to communicate with. Now that you have finished reading this book, you are one step closer to having a successful relationship that begins online and extends offline. Don't wait, take some action now! The most successful people in the world have a supporting partner to help them through life.

Finally, if you discovered at least one thing that has helped you or that you think would be beneficial to someone else, be sure to take a few seconds to easily post a quick positive review. As an author, your positive feedback is desperately needed. Your highly valuable five star reviews are like a river of golden joy flowing through a sunny forest of mighty trees and beautiful flowers! *To do your good deed in making the world a better place by helping others with your valuable insight, just leave a nice review.*

My Other Books and Audio Books
www.AcesEbooks.com

Health Books

ULTIMATE HEALTH SECRETS

HEALTH

Strategies For Dieting, Eating Healthy, Exercising,
Losing Weight, The Mediterranean Diet,
Strength Training, And All About Vitamins,
Minerals, And Supplements

Ace McCloud

ENERGY
ULTIMATE ENERGY

Discover How To Increase
Your Energy Levels
Using The Best All Natural
Foods, Supplements
And Strategies For A Life
Full Of Abundant Energy

Ace McCloud

RECIPE BOOK

The Best Food Recipes
That Are Delicious, Healthy,
Great For Energy And Easy To Make

Ace McCloud

MASSAGE THERAPY

TRIGGER POINT THERAPY
ACUPRESSURE THERAPY
Learn The Best Techniques For
Optimum Pain Relief And Relaxation

Ace McCloud

LOSE WEIGHT

**THE TOP 100 BEST WAYS
TO LOSE WEIGHT QUICKLY AND HEALTHILY**

Ace McCloud

FATIGUE
OVERCOME CHRONIC FATIGUE

Discover How To Energize
Your Body & Mind So
That You Can Bring
The Energy & Passion
Back Into Your Life

Ace McCloud

Peak Performance Books

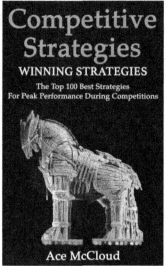

Be sure to check out my audio books as well!

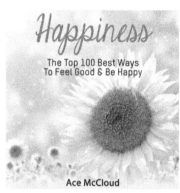
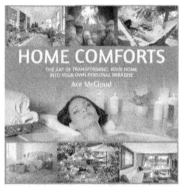

Check out my website at: www.AcesEbooks.com for a complete list of all of my books and high quality audio books. I enjoy bringing you the best knowledge in the world and wish you the best in using this information to make your journey through life better and more enjoyable! **Best of luck to you!**

CPSIA information can be obtained
at www.ICGtesting.com
Printed in the USA
BVOW07s2259100417
480817BV00020B/111/P